To the Occupant

To the Occupant

EMMA NEALE

OTAGO

For Danny

Published by Otago University Press
Level 1, 398 Cumberland Street
Dunedin, New Zealand
university.press@otago.ac.nz
www.otago.ac.nz/press

First published 2019
Copyright © Emma Neale

Editor: Anna Hodge
Design/layout: Fiona Moffat
Author photograph: Jim Tannock

Front cover: Nick Austin, *Travelling Envelope #2*, 2012 (detail), acrylic on newspaper, 575 x 785mm.
Courtesy of the artist and Hopkinson Mossman

Printed in New Zealand by Southern Colour Print, Dunedin

CONTENTS

To the Occupant

A body, such a ponderous thing
to drag along a life in

this coffin-fat cabinet
the mind-candle
push-pedals around
and such tiny perforations
to peer through
at the drip-drop
greeny-diamond world ...

But you, still new,
mind wide,
lick it, taste it,
lollop through it
blithe as a rabbit
a-whiffle at berry canes

show us again
how lightly to shoulder
these old bone crates,
remind us we are wrong
when we long
to lay them down.

I

A Room that Held the Sea

Courtship

He wooed me many ways: tried everything from lending books to night-dancing, blood starry with lager. We talked, yet it wasn't working. So he left the country, asking if he could keep in touch.

His letters—handwritten—soon arrived. He laughs when I say this, but it was seduction by punctuation. As if each semi-colon was someone leaning forward, head bubbling with the future; or perhaps an athlete, leaping for the catch. Such elegance and rhythm.

Bud and stalk; sun and moon; hook and sinker. A bottle that's popped its cork. Or even egg and ecstatic sperm, pre-fusion.

Wild Peregrinations

From the look-out point
of sleep's edge
the years spread back
with all the pinprick fires and dark clutches
of an old, uneasy settlement.

The thoughts watch themselves,
the way one falcon acts silent sentinel
to another across the blue whisper
of desolate distances.

Then—as if it believes
its moon-washed, grass-gold hide
will be ample camouflage—
a dart, a jink,
an erratic dash and back-dash:
hope's wild peregrinations,
love's blood-sweet liqueur
crammed beneath its skin.

Wedding Kiss

The four-year-old gasps
averts his face
scrunches his eyes shut tight:
love is an onion
desire the knife.

Morning Song

Gramps stole eggs, green seeds of song, from their nests
to show us wonder; hairline cracks ran
our sooky hearts as we watched the robbed mothers fly home.
He cradled fallen fledglings in his palm, quoted
Thrush's eggs ... like little low heavens, and
Bare ruined choirs where late the sweet birds sang
then barked, 'Who wrote those?'
When we didn't know:
'What d'they *teach* you these days?'

He kept army hours, was formal with our fathers:
hellos were handshakes as if manners
meant even sons' love should be held at arm's length.
Yet, his face a white wilted poppy,
he forbade the word *hate*
as yelled at brothers or sisters
over Yahtzee or Scrabble cheats,
at garden hoses poked down trousers,
or whose turn it was for more *sucky* chores.

He had seen hate. Had lived inside it.
Knew its cattle trucks, lice-run bunks,
its thorn-crowned wires, borne its hunger
over borders and weeks, stepped over its corpses
to follow orders, eaten its soup afloat
with leather threads, and, once, a donkey's eye.
Taken prisoner, he'd doctored the war-interred,
separated off the sick for hospital camps.
Where the well were sent, he couldn't bear to say.

All through his house and daily he whistled 'Morning Has Broken';
heard so often *blackbird has spoken* stopped meaning birdsong:
it meant Gramps and damp tea towels; thin coffee cups and saucers
glazed with flowers that could be owls; owls that could be flowers,
as in the Garner novel I doubt he ever read;
his hours too crowded with the history books he scoured,
still on the trail fifty years later
for what drives human
to its own dread perimeters.

Praise for them springing fresh from the word
meant tales of war curtly turned
down byways of jokes, witty anecdotes:
for we were only the children of his children;
there was no translation from *lived* to *tale*
that could ever ...
those random, horrifying odds
that gave us all his sun-speckled kitchen ...
better not re-count them.

Better warble down the past's wind
mine is the sunlight, mine is the morning.
We grinned, raised eyebrows at its no-fail return;
praise with elation, praise every morning
the tune all whiskered trill, all rheumy-eyed wink
as he'd pop a dishcloth over his shoulder,
a clown's epaulette; *praise for the sweetness ...*

But the bassline silence seeping
ominous as horizons blazing in the dark;
we heard that, too: the thrum of how our own luck shone.
How improbable the emaciated man
told by Nazi guards he would be shot at dawn
should have found this reprieve at all:

family banter in the kitchen,
tea towels flicked like circus whips;
retired GP, buffing crockery, fortissimo on key;
even at home smuggling single smokes
up his cardigan sleeve; admitting nothing
when they dropped at our feet:
just cocking a blackbird's peck-quick eye,
slipping the cigarette back up his cuff
and whistling, piercingly, on.

A Room that Held the Sea

Over cocktails, perhaps, or card games, or at book club in the shared day-room
of the small port-town retirement home, although on a street with no view of
the sea,

a woman told my grandfather of the day she walked into the room
where her mother wept and rocked, as if on a deck on a wind-lashed sea,
half-crazed with disbelief, barely aware she was in her own living-room.
Living-room itself sounded almost crass, as its corners seeped with a red-blind sea,
despair's deep tide staining mouth and mind so its curse fixed the image of that room
for good, for worse, in the young girl's memory. Through it she could never
again see

this spring-kindled world; five words nailed up their own dank room,
they rang bitter-clear: 'It should have been you.' Her mother forgivably at sea;
yet cruel—unforgivably. Kinder to have denied entry to that plunging room
where she tried to drag back from shock's current, treacherous as a rip at sea;
back from the news that sucked all light from the room.
One young daughter drowned while swimming in an easy summer's sea.
The other stood, hair still tangle-damp, limbs glittered with tawny sand, a dozen
rooms

in the wish-castle of self slammed shut: turned dust-patina'd ghost embassy.
Even at 93, once-translator, ex-diplomat's widow, her smile a tern's quick tilt in the
sky's vast room,
she swore her life story was, 'My sister died. My mother wished it was me.' Eyes
grey as wake on winter seas;
family love a lost Atlantis: anoxic as cold marbled rooms, undersea.

'my mother in this way mixing me wings and tongue'

after Paula Green

Mint's fresh breath on all its haka tongues   marigolds   white pebbles
      battered wooden chair   geraniums   fruit canes   lemon verbena
chives and thyme   and from a blue jug on a red Formica table   a waft of
      memory   rides on fine fragrance   a woman says   ah look
sweet peas   darling   you know   though you are knee-high to a
footstool   busy with your trike   going round and round the clothesline
      aware of something good and solid to your left that you are saving up to look at
later   something as anchoring as bread and butter or a hand-sewn rabbit
in swallow-tailed coat   that her voice somehow means   *wild enchantment*
      it's sweet sorcery and milk spiked with fey   beauty calls for pause   soon
it will dissolve   as elusive as the silver moths that cast quick shadow darts
on your skin   with the cool sensation of water   though see the sky is dry

So you stop   and you plunge your face in   and the scent takes you
somewhere like stained glass   cream lace fountains and maze walks in towering
hedges   somewhere like white picnic cloths and wicker baskets   burnished ringlets
      forest tangle   centaurs   sprites   dryads   a small elfin thing hiding under
nasturtium   rangiora leaves written on with sticks, call it bush paper
      barefoot topknot man with pounamu in his hand   pixies suckling at
the flowers' thin teats   green tree shade tunnels   careful leonine saunter
      bird cry-cascade   and it all melts down   over the years
      to white ankle socks   scuffed sandals   metal trike   her brushed-cotton
green zip-up dress   ample hold   bare arms   the full voice of
this brown-haired woman saying   in that slow   though urgent   way   ah
      look   *sweet peas*   darling

So Buttoned Up

after Stephen Bett

First time in my god
damned life I forgot
my name and when
you said it, it went
sherbet-wise inside
the tiny wires
of each thought-capillary
every ringing filament
streamed like candy dazzle
lights in the rain
so how to maintain
equipoise on its leggy stems
without once thinking of how
the wine glasses we held were
modelled on a French queen's
breasts and then *nek minnit*
as they didn't say then
(we're old-timers, baby)
you were asking me
and what do you do
for a living?
When the truth was
I'd been in some wise dead
until my name fled
and you chased it
while I feigned
not to know
certain facts such as
the very pulse of its note
had just been breath

warmed beneath where
those shirt buttons sat
obedient and still
as small bald monks
meditating
patiently
upon
detachment.

Memorial Service

Twenty years
of sorely missed;
I thumb your number
into my contacts list
so the new phone displays
your resurrection day:
Love's Name—saved.

Cut Price

At the grocery store we choose the shortest queue.
On the conveyor belt sit five mini-tins of cat food
with two identical budget spice-shakers.

We're behind a man whose skin is pale as lunch paper
and whose jersey droops from his shoulders
as if it's still being knitted
from the needles of his bones.

He startles when the check-out operator says
there's a two-for-one deal on that cat-meat brand.
The man urges us to take his place
before he shambles back
as fast as shuffle-can
to the pet food aisle.

But we can't.
We wait—
because we do have a cat,
although today we don't buy cat food
and the children have never
had to think so hard
about what taste might hunker
behind a mask of white pepper.

Will our small joys be only their ancestors?

That day, beside the sea's sleep-rumpled sheets
the sun had leapt from to arrive on time,
there were chickens laughing as if they'd woken
to tell each other outrageous dreams;
there were bushes bursting to tell you their purple,
honeysuckle trumpets miming fanfare along the street,
a clam-white boat with blue-silk lining,
a shag drying its glossy korowai
on honeycombed, biscuit-coloured rock,
driftwood sticks like Bo-Peep crooks,
a wilding apple tree leaning away
from one small rātā's red cliff-edge shout,
a flock of oyster-catchers tapping bullet points in the sand;
seaweed fronds like the hair of selkies
diving for taniwha gleam;
hills the sad colour of straw
though the cicadas urged on
the bellbird cabaret;
and at the watermark a black stone
like a carved ceremonial urn.

All of it laps at memory's coves
like the lines of folk songs
our children might sing—
of the safedays,
from the bygones.

Warning

This item
contains images
an audience may
find distressing.

A thin child in clothes that don't quite fit: mid-shin trousers and red short sleeves
although the autumn morning is charity cold, his back swaddled in foreign air, face
down against the white winding cloth of the shallows, cheeks pressed to wet sand
like a baby burrowed into the scent trace of lavender only please won't someone
tuck love's covers over his shoulders, don't stay in that twist, little one, your back
and neck will ache when you wake, the sea is an unschooled nurse to let you lie
that way, the white hygiene gloves of the soldier such small care who lifts your
drifted spine, he is trained not to weep so he can still see this shore hell, navigate
the sink holes of all dread terrain, trained not to mistake you for his own son, to
stifle the cries *Allahu Akbar, grant forgiveness.*
In his arms, horror's answer.

This era
contains events
we must
find appalling.

Called

It is October in Dunedin.
Rhododendrons fan out flounced skirts;
magnolias, magnanimous with their moon-cool glow,
light the path south so the sun stirs us early;
although the river, the creek boulders,
the city's cinched green belt, still hold the cold
like an ice store's packed-down snow.

The days shiver with filaments
of ua kōwhai: soft rain that dampens paths,
shakes loose carpets of white stamens, yellow flowers
bruised and trodden like flimsy foil cornets.
School holidays send out falling, silvery arcs
of children's sky-flung laughter; our bodies drink it in
as if love's parched ground sore needs this watering.

Yet the radio stays hunched in the kitchen corner
hard grey clot in the light's fine arteries
muttering its tense bulletins;
and as if they sense this late spring still harbours
frost's white wreck, or some despotic harm abroad
seeps too near, our sons more than anything want
their old games: secret codes, invisible ink, velvet cloaks;
hide 'n' seek in public gardens' clefts and coves—

and again, again, can we tell them again

the chapters of how they first appeared
in the long, blurred myths we are entangled in;
kingfisher-blue wells of their eyes a-gleam
as if they know how much all adults withhold.
They want us to go back deeper, to when

we both were star-spill, sea-flume, spirits,
only belatedly woman, man, climbing up from a shore
feathered in sand black and soft as ash,
driven by some gravid magnetism towards each other

in case we changed to birds, lizards, trees,
or back to sea-salt borne by wind;
an urge clear as hunger coursing the cells' deep helix
to complete this alteration, half-bury and re-germinate
the fleet molecules of self, so we could run our mortal hands
the small, kind way along the children's plush skins,
learn, pulse on pulse, their true, human names.
Yes, we must go back and back; as if to swear
even to this dread epoch's wild, original innocence.

October 2015

The Belt

How could they ever love anyone else
after what he had done?

Listened to that woman whose voice graunched
like a spoon that tries to drag the pattern off the plate
when even the broth scrapings are gone.

Took them into the forest as if already
the appetite of wolves was merely sleepy milktime fable.

Tied a dead branch loose against a tree
so it tapped in the wind like the sound of his axe,
mimic of love's vigilance labouring on,
seeing clear into a shared future
that it would build and warm:
icy gaps under the doors barricaded;
night fire singing like their lost blood-mother after wine.

But he had gone back to that other,
to sup with her, they guessed,
his mouth on her the way they had once glimpsed:
like a dog knocking its bowl across the floor as it drank,
the woman clutching along the mattress,
the pale loaf of her rising to him,
their father dropping back as if he was her windfall plum;

while the crackle and buzz of hunger in the children's heads
turned them outside early, to nibble on leaves, bark,
even the boy's brown leather belt,
which made them wonder and whisper
about rumours of magic: for week by week
the belt's dark, parched tongue lengthened,
when all else around them waned, marked by famine.

Big Bad

She cried wolf but she was the wolf
so she slit sad's bellyskin
and stones of want rolled out.

She cried lack—and she was the lack
so she stitched up sad's bellyskin
but more wolf leapt out.

She cried wolf till wolf was all cried out
and up skipped those stones
like knock-kneed urchykins

to finger-feed her humble pie
smooth her voice like teacher's chalk
soften her palms like baker's flour

and those stones they smacked
their lips and sang,
yes, yes Miss Cat-skin,
you'll do for the kitchen;
please, please Miss Wolf-skin,
won't we all do for love?

The Local Pool

Turn a corner, into air tangy with chlorine. The smell removes memory's stopper and an anxious genie swims out. What about the turquoise of a small town pool? What about concrete, dark with Rorschach marks that wet bodies left behind after boys egged on and watched?

Police, phoned by a passerby: the next day, when their own girls cried 'See ya!' over pop-radio falsetto, did the cops saloon-door from their bathrooms, half-Santaed with soap, then gruff up quick hugs, foam-chins hooked over their daughters' shoulders, to hide fuel-lines of dread in their eyes?

The mothers of the pool-girl's friends: did they slash open packets, shove cupboards shut, slam on about hemlines and torn black tights peep-showing lucky pennies of skin, because grown women can't just wish-link pinkies, to ward off a suburb's sons?

The girl's friends, asked by social workers to tell when she skipped classes, because she had to get back on track, mustn't let one summer dusk haunt her with that boy crisping her open, peeling her back like the winding-key on a tin of imported sweets—did those friends stop reporting because tears skirred free as she begged *please don't*? Or because they learned she'd agreed to meet the boy again, at a bus shelter's cold bunker, and the red folded mystery of how a wound could drag her back to its own start was too confusing? As disorienting as the acrid smoke they heard about later, when a schoolbag, schoolbooks, stockings, wasp-striped school tie, were soaked in art-room turps and set alight, as

a girl prayed for flames to leap a pine plantation's firebreak, hive for the new subdivision and one blue house, its yard junked with bikes and a boy's outgrown clobber, slung into trash bags slumped limp as drunks.

Minor Goddess

With baby-tooth-marked wooden spoon and porridge pot,
her diadem of elastic band and tussocky, sleep-mussed bed-hair,
her nightdress hemmed in god-pups fighting fisticuffs,

our neighbour's a lesser-known goddess
of the linoleum and cutlery drawer, of leftovers and small, fleet spurts of joy, which,
should you make the right fond offerings, might dart in you, too.

On these frost-moored mornings, she leans out from her warm, yellow cove of
homespun heaven, scented with coffee and cinnamon,
mucky with toast crumbs honeyhooked to rumpled cotton,

and above a street white with seeds of ice, she scoops scraps from the pot, spoons
them to a window-side perch, nailed on like a bird's spare room;
fills a chipped china cup with sugar-water—

And lo, from snow-bitter air, wrist-warm oats and kitchen-sink nectar,
she kindles song-crop and wing-flicker: waxeyes, darting daubs of green and pewter;
tūī, sleek as puma, beaks noble as Horus, white poi throat-feathers proud Adam's
apples.

Avid prophets, their high cascades, *See! See!*
summon up more wonder; they seed
this blended, jostling flock:

blackbirds, sparrows, finches, korimako, thrushes, starlings, kererū,
birds, birds, birds, all bank and quiver, ruffle and hosanna, as if they love,
how they love, her mothered-up, midlife, sleepily stove-singed mild oats.

II

'So Sang a Little Clod of Clay'

Harwood Beach Walk: Eavesdropping

A man says, 'Do you know him?'
A woman answers, 'Oh yes,
he was one of my first loves.'

The man laughs
his firm, dry correction:
'There can only ever be one first.'

Yet the coppery flax plant rocks
its slim black seed keels
in the wind's arms;

a cabbage tree practises arpeggios of light;
on the harbour's roiling waters
white fire flares, then douses; flares again.

The peninsula hills sleep, leonine,
as the tūī's aria marks and remarks
the arc of its territory.

In the mind's ear, the sweet selective amnesia
of Lilburn's 'Moths and Candles' newly beautiful
each time it's played.

Like the roots of myth,
dark stones exposed by tidal ebb
bloom, uncurve their necks:
swans lifting from the creel of sleep.

Yes, hasn't she caught it—
that we are wet clay
in the moment's hands;

and so much more so
for each love's
momentous admission
breaking, remaking us in its form.

Doorway

On the pavement outside the famous patisserie
a slender, chignon-haired woman sits inside her fortress

of backpack, tote bags, suitcases
which she arranges and rearranges

with the worn sobriety of a new mother
or a nurse in a recovery-ward hover.

Her palms rest on the luggage temples
as she whispers numbers: times or temperatures;

she fingers across pockets and linings
to check sutures, swellings, compressions,

now tallies the bags with the panic
of a teacher herding pupils because *this is not a drill*

and she is strained enough, painfully thin enough,
for us to halt our hurry, offer food, money, enquiries

but she grows fierce in her count, as if leucocytes, nebulae,
ghosts or tempests hinge on this, she chants charms,

colours and figures to hold the bristling *bourrage*
of our bodies, voices and faces at bay.

She pivots, moves and re-patterns the cases,
follows some complex internal schematics;

frets at her soapstone choker as if to lift the hex
memory's shadow projects on tomorrow—

so we find we turn to our watches, mobiles, to check places
we said we'd be, friends we promised to see;

we mutter and singsong, draw our children as close
as the blue-skinned passports nestled at our hips;

repeat names, dates, flights: anchors, mantras,
bulwarks to staunch this internal mounting frantic keening disarray.

Mère-mare

Last night in my sleep
my baby's father came
to take him away from me.

I had borne a boy
I was forbidden to hold
though his mouth was sere and sore
and golden colostrum welled in me
like the cells' own cry for water.

I had done some terrible thing—
and as I slowly woke to it,
groping for knowledge as if for watch or lamp,
the baby gazed at me
with ancient desperation;
yet flat, dim shapes dragged me back
as my breasts wept runnels of milk's white lava;
and the new father spoke
with the crackle of plastic,
swore the new mother could never
bear to see me; said I'd signed a pact
to render my child unto them
as if the body were merely an ice cube mould
that had only to heat and flex a little
to release its self-compacted pockets
of piquant, enigmatic sweetness.

When I truly woke
and both real sons crept in close beside me,
tousled heads bunting the crook of my arms, my neck
like young steers remembering their udder-honey,

even then, the scalpel of loss hooked deep, scored deeper—
even now, something naked, lowing and primate haunts here

terrified of what truths speak through dreams.

'So Sang a Little Clod of Clay'

—William Blake

When it hurts, but she doesn't say
When it dulls, but he still gives praise
When she bites, but he refuses rage
and he walks free, though she stays.

When they wait through blunt dismay
though they ache as the children play,
this is tread and bootgrind
this is hope's hard labour
this is the heart's ripe savour
this is the sting of healing
this is the rope of time—

and love is dust
ignited
in fleet, golden murmuration.

Tone Poem

The korimako descant | the fine white china lid of the sky | the pounamu twist pendant |
on the hitchhiking librarian;
the sound of cars speeding | on wet tarmac in the distance |
the wide coastal state highway | sea-wrack strewn shore | stumbling grey knee bones
of the rocks | all made it seem in sweet season |

The fast angular electric guitar | the chartreuse lens of the unopened wine |
some Jeep parked in a side alley | the metallic tap of an office worker's heels |
the coronets of fresh dew | held high on the ferns' brows |
even the high thin whine of head cold | like a phone in a villa's back corridor |
beneath the stained-glass soar of the bird's tiny coloratura from power lines, trees ⨪|
together made the days carry | a sharp citrus tang of the real |

As if the man | so clearly branched with doubt |
about you | were merely incidental | and that low blood thrum |
(through tussock's shudder, | through salt glister of damp sand, |
through fleshy slap of wooden spoon in batter, | through snug of lost in hand, |
through sun-pitched song strains, | through thick fog scarves round coastal throats) |
‖: was the earth's own *cantabile* | along time's deep capillaries :‖

Resurrection

Remember the Magic 8-Ball fortune-teller toys
the other kids had in America?

You'd ask a question, then shake the water-filled black globe,
wait for the printed dice inside to drift up with its prediction.

Remember itself now mirrors shake and tilt:
first it brings an ink-dark blank, then up floats a looming, partial view.

Something agitates us: say, the pop-song cheese
in a hotel lobby that seeds restless irritation

then falls through chords that bend the day's snow-dulled air;
so that soon, oscillating under the song's surface, comes memory's bright flotsam

back from when there was a father who was together with a mother;
a little, giggly sister; a rented house with Merryweather steamers on the wallpaper;

a rabbit called Erik the Red; roller skates with blue ankle boots;
a trust we thought as tough as the dimes we'd bite like gold doubloons.

Or perhaps a jolt comes while reading in a café, from a novel's scene that hurtles
a grandfather's war stories to the fore, horror as visible

as that fortune-ball's printed messages. It obliterates the lacquer
of civilisation over us, the gentle Sri Lankan waiter with garnet ring,

the coffee bill he presents with a grace and politesse
that the charge barely pays obeisance for. Or like that insult spat on screen

at a stranger who accidentally jostled another in a bus—
fucking sand-bunny, go back to where you came from—that has me fret,

then later turn, mid-work, to Google a name I'd not thought it possible to trace.
Her soft, eight-year-old face, white ankle socks, long skirt

sway up from the past; quiet ally in alien schoolyards, wrenched back to Iran,
moments, it seemed, before political crisis hit; no time to comprehend

nor pledge goodbyes; letters never arrived; days turned
to clotted buttermilk spilling, never unspilling, the confusion meant

I hardly knew how I came to stand up, bull-headed, white-fisted,
at yet another school: little antipodean transient,

bawling at a thistle-haired boy who'd replayed the parental hate
he thought to dignify as News; and though I scarcely understood the words *shah*,
                                                            ayatollah,

fury's particles arced. 'It is not *all Iranians*.
It's about *governments*. I had a friend. Her name was Roshi.

'She's gone, but her family did nothing wrong.'
Her date-dark eyes brimmed with premature wisdom,

yet her smile travels decades unbroken; she the only child
to speak to me on my first day in migrant skin.

And now, dazzled, frantic, as if clutching rails on a plunging deck,
I'm scanning the streaming oracles of LinkedIn, Facebook,

crying out to time's indifferent captains, *Wait! She's alive.*
Roshi Givechi is alive!

Teen Genie

Against the solemn tiers of male choristers
dressed in waiters' black and white,
red binders of their song sheets held aloft
so the scene serves a formal music for the eye,

one tall, sweet, lanky teen calmly queens it
onto stage; perches at the glittery drum kit;
invited to give these good old boys a rock beat
for their concert's one 'edgy' modern piece.

His pale-blue denim jacket, skinny jeans, DM boots,
lip gloss, mascara, the dark blond, afro-dahlia of his hair
stir squawks and eddies of disturbance in the audience
as if a toddler mock airbombs a flock of drowsy pigeons.

Yet his long spine still straightens for the count;
he hits the rhythm's clip, smooth and tight—
so at the song's end, after storms of applause,
whooped delight, and above the widening pool of quiet

even the thin, sky-pitched whistles
conjured from someone's failing hearing-aids
seem like the cries of tiny, pink-throated larks
carolling jubilation.

Tag

From the tangle of trees
by the Warrender Street steps
near where city council crews have been deleting
the *fuck-cunts* and dick pics sprayed on the path,
sharper than the *doof-doof* of the stereo
from a student party in the valley's dank trench,
comes the sound of castanets.

Someone drunk has peeled away from the party
to climb this high; camouflaged now
as sky puzzle, green-stitched twig-work
so all we can see is sycamore sway, azaleas,
rhododendrons in their flamenco blaze.

They clatter again, *tik-tik-ticka-chicka!*
Closer now, it's clear we'd got it wrong;
it is the hard bead rattle
as someone preps and shakes aerosol paint.

Doggeding up the steps we scan
the ragged branch and bloomscape
for what little punk might be so half-cut
they'd even graffiti-cuss the trees—

ah quick-quick-look, there there he is
that small sleek agile man
in his hooded, beaked, silken onesie—

trickster korimako
bellbird, mimic bird, can-bird:
in great neon streams now
he tags the air with song—

bird iz here! bird lovez azaleaz! bird lovez birdz!

Two Birds Billing

>x x<

Desire

Be rid of this red ire

                                Sire.
                    rise,
            and

It Goes Without Saying

*

—

...

Aubade

After the bird's first small enquiries
CDEC? CDEC?
love turns, soft awake
makes embrace song's corollary.

Sheetweb Spider

For weeks, a spider sits on the white ceiling
a small, dark star of muscle and mind.

We could navigate
the boat of our bed by her
if we ever wake marooned
or terrified by
the salt-blue expanse
of time and tide beyond
the known tomorrows
that wait for no mantra
from any of broken us, my love.

The spider hunches;
silent nun
her white prayer flags
spun on thin air

a Zen pin
on the light's cartography—

hold this stillness
until this stillness holds.

Here,
you are.

Blue Rubato

Outside an inner-city high school
near a gutter glum with rubbish
(licked yoghurt pots, brown fruit peel)
the itinerant music teacher
scalp polished as clarinet keys
bends slightly to the side while his palms lift
as if to pray for just one pupil steeped in genius.

His mouth puckers a little and—
Whoa, he's got it bad, can't contain
desire's blood tango: side-steps in a swoon,
air-kisses an absent lover,
hallucinates fragrance on orchid-smooth skin ...

Wrong. As we walk in closer,
his hands adjust position
so he can hold the world's smallest oboe:
as we pass, we tilt our heads to catch
his spontaneous street solo,
pianissimo as the kazoo
of a bee mid-air-doodle—
nope. Hey-ho. He's ducked aside
to protect a Zippo from the wind.
His cigarette blows a blue rubato.

Trainee Emo

His heart feels as if it swings its socks and shoes in one hand only to discover prickle-grass under its pale and tender feet

No, his heart feels like a pink geranium craning to see into the gardener's window, just after half its branches have been hacked off

No, his heart is the black security strap on a trampoline's edge-padding: dangling, growing a thin coat of moss: essential, but ignored

No, his heart is like a stinging eyelid he can't scratch for fear he'll smudge his eyeliner and draw his family's attention to it: as if they know anything about him

No, his heart feels like the large itchy lumps brought on by eating something delicious but highly allergenic

No, don't be an arse, his heart feels like the smudge on the wall where his sister hit a bluebottle with a Nerf bullet: unbelievably sick and fluky death

No, his heart feels like the dog-eared page the ideal reader actually never turns back to

> You know, his heart could go on like this forever,
> but the aroma of his mother's *croque monsieur*
> serenades on its irresistible pan-pipes
> through the light-gap under his door
>
> so he Rapunzels himself down
> from his towering melancholy,
> vows to treat all family jokes
> as he would the tear-sting of Tabasco:
> swallow the burning words.
> Asks quietly for a glass of cow's.

Sonnet for Mr Ponting, HOD Maths & Economics

I upset Mr Ponting today with my immature facetious reaction to eating in economics class like a budgie.
I upset Mr Ponting today with my immature facetious reaction to eating in economics class like a budgie.
I upset Mr Ponting today with my immature facetious reaction to eating in economics class like a budgie.
I upset Mr Ponting today with my immature facetious reaction to eating in economics class like a budgie.
I upset Mr Ponting today with my immature facetious reaction to eating in economics class like a budgie.
I upset Mr Ponting today with my immature facetious reaction to eating in economics class like a budgie.
I upset Mr Ponting today with my immature facetious reaction to eating in economics class like a budgie.
I upset Mr Ponting today with my immature facetious reaction to eating in economics class like a budgie.

But I'd probably upset him more if I dared show the edits
Mum scrawls on all the lines he sets for detention
(today, blunt eyebrow pencil in 'Midnight Burlesque' all over my loose-leaf)
or worse, if he saw the slurs she scrawls on their reverse.
Not everyone's as gaga on grammar as she is: not even teachers.
Don't think I'm meek. Just resigned. Money geeks like him have already scored the earth.

Distance

It was the first spring the child realised
he had seen other springs
and had grown his own memories.
'So—not very long till you are old!' he cried
with a quarter smile, flummoxed
by his own smug-sad wisdom

and the pain that flew in
through the mind's skylight
was so swift and silvering,
I plunged my nose into the magnolia's bowl,
I plunged it again to the pale spray of wild plum,
its flowers the size of the metal snap-domes
on a baby's stretch 'n' grow;
then asked, 'Do they have a scent? Can you tell?'

He copied. 'Mmmm, they do. It's beautiful,
but it's very, very faint—as if we're looking
out of the backs of our minds.
Or feel it from a hill very far beside the sky.'

As if we can only know some things
at a distance. From years away, say.
Or the granular, woven light of a page.

Small Wonder

Our youngest, back home from his nana's,
catapults himself into the kitchen on the sprung elastic
of a secret he says he can never, ever tell.

I set a knife aside, towel my hands dry,
clasp him close and say, '*Hey, hey,*
little one, hey?'

He pushes in hard at the sides of his mouth
as the blue-green fire of his irises
brims and flickers, swells and burns.

He pounces at his own impulsive tongue
so it's trapped between two knuckles
the way a cat will paw-slam a skink;

and again with both hands
in some odd, kitschy copy of an Edvard Munch,
he stretches down his bottom lip

—so I'm braced for a tale
of rapscallion shenanigans: muck and break,
sweet-thievery from Nana's biscuit tins;

felt-pen sunglasses and beer can
scribbled on a Jesus bookmark,
or water-pistol *bulls-eyed!* at her corkboard

with its ancient Xeroxed articles
that frown, 'Would YOU want monkeys for uncles?'
or warn, 'Harry Potter: Gateway Drug to Satan'.

'Did some trouble come up at Nana's?'
'*No!*' and his wail says he's battled the urge to tell
for the entire afternoon …

I have to promise not to laugh.
Not to pass it on.
I have to promise again, *promise*.

I have to close the door, yes, bend down,
so he can whisper inside his hands
that are cupped now like a cloche

to ward off admonishment's frost,
block disbelief's
orange wire-cutter beaks,

protect the pale-pink nimbus
of his secret
as it buds, opens.

Bilingual

At our seven-year-old's school, there's a new pupil.
His name is Huiseong Song: Korean for bright star.

'That's cool!' our son exclaims.
'He sounds like the song of songs,

'the most singing-est of songs!'
Our tousled pipistrelle in ripped black jeans,

he shins up a tree and cries, 'Hey, Huiseong! *Hi!*'
Joy's echolocation, afternoon serenade

in the playground the children have christened,
like some old-time ship, *The Adventure*.

Below the climbing frame's mock-rigging, moored
in caution's vertigo, his mother confides

fear's limbo: for Huiseong knows no English.
Yet—see how he close-reads hands and feet

for *grip and swing, scoot and climb,*
drop and land and run; the children's step and leap

are smoke, are sails, are flags;
are pale-gold flashes marked on black bark,

sticks laid like arrows on fresh mud,
light brush strokes on day's blue scroll.

Just one week later, when I ask, 'How's Huiseong?'
Our son grins, finds him, cups his elbow;

with an 'On your marks, get set, *go!*'
side by side they run and rise;

they clamber, they tree-hide,
they *You're In*, they *Not-It*,

agile under leaf-steeples,
limber in sun-time,

fluent, already, in the fleet code-switch
between a wilding self and first other-kin.

Dark Glass

Against all the winter mind has dreaded: spring again.
We worry, is it too early, will it thrive?
The foamhead of blossoms rushes up the dark, glassy branches
as if festive Prosecco has been spilled well before the wedding, the win.

Optimism, too, stupidly, biologically brims, as I hurry into the city dusk
expecting young crowds tipsy with what they think is wine,
though the zing is really the fumes and flint of their own swift blood.

The stances of a man and a woman in a doorway
short the night as if hidden wires touch—
though there is ample space between them.
They radiate something the way a snake's hooded head does.
Or the scorpion's curved tail.
Animal. Angular. Their voices rise higher. Blunt but chopped.

What I catch is you *said*,
I *never*, you *always*, you *can't*.
And in the middle, against the shop's boarded-up door,
there is a small girl calling, 'Mummy, no! Daddy, stop!'
And the parents slip strange quick sly looks over their shoulders
though there is plenty of history left in the clip, they don't stop—

you *just*, I *told* you, you *didn't*,

the same accusations
that corner me here,
shame-crouched
clicking through keys like a rosary,
because I did not stop, turn back, or speak.
I did not.

My Aunt's Story

She tells me of when she and her twin were only eight,
on a family visit south to meet their own brand-new aunt,

a young émigrée due to arrive and settle
in a small antipodean riverside town.

As Sunday-crisp and silken as rosettes, ribbons,
the townsfolk gathered on the station platform

all there with fresh-picked posies, handmade signs,
to greet my great-uncle's Welsh war bride.

Sun-struck gossamer, expectation itself seemed afloat, alight,
as both twins clutched confetti, watched the train arrive.

Yet even before my aunt's own foreign aunt
had stepped her way along the narrow aisle

they saw her infants through the carriage window.
My grandmother warned, urgent and low,

'Hide your confetti, children. Quickly. Hide it,'
then hugged them tight from pressing forward.

Horror's echo in gaunt and bone. The almost unspeakable real.
Another aunt, in whispered shock: *But they look like Belsen babies.*

So as when the starved, to heal,
must first be served the plainest meal

the bouquets, confetti, the banners enamelled with joy
were lowered, concealed; for now they seemed to blare and bloat,

too much, too rich, too soon for history's
Blitz-shocked, harrowed envoys.

Still

When young, I used to think
a solitary on a public bench

must be mournfully isolate,
soul full-sore from thought's arid trek,

gaze plunged inwards, sifting the past's thick clag
to try to mine again the ember-gleam

of optimism, or love's gold-foiled veins.
Yet now the world feels city-crammed, fierce-frantic,

a disco dystopia drugged by greed-eats-need,
a singleton moored in thought on a park bench

seems a gifted votary of silence,
a living icon of some secret

south seas paradise
of the stilled and quiet mind.

Camellia Trees

When she was five she went boldly into the world
all on her not-telling alone; hiked a great distance,
brave, she thought it, to break out of the dust-cloth hours
of boredom; in her head, a small voice sang
she walked ache-rs and ache-rs; ache-rs and ache-rs she roamed;
sturdily she forged into the soft and secret gloam made below
the camellia trees discovered by her travels;
crawled into their green cave hiddenly;
crouched under the crinkled pink fabrics,
afloat on the loam-sweet scent, soil plush as rabbit paws,
the small beetles and ladybirds trusting enough
to adorn her fingers like mobile jewels—
emerald, garnet, onyx; the colours too
of the quiet, the privacy, the dusk,
the benevolence of trees stooped low
like close angelic attendants in old church windows
shiny as thin-sucked lemon drops, barley twists—
yes, she would like to turn back even now,
although she guesses in truth the trees
were just along a neighbourhood fence;
knows she could only stand there,
elephantine, sigh-worn, mind sleep-grained
as when woken too soon by children
who clamour to open their dollhouse again;
the taste of straw and mash coating her mouth,
the ache in her joints of hill climbs, sway-spine,
someone in the years' long night
must have slipped her into harness, behind her a cart
that cries with ragged chattels, the laden cases
of *these are your days, darlings,*
you must shoulder them, shoulder them.

Withdrawn

It is not within the scope of this poem
to discuss the failure of successive governments
to address the glaring discrepancies
between all the different weights and shades
of human pain—

but suffice to say that today,
on George Street in Dunedin, 2017,
I saw a thin young man
in a sleeping bag
on top of a flattened cardboard box
with a disposable cup for coins at his side

and he couldn't look up
when he thanked us
for the twelve-pack of fresh bread rolls
we'd had to walk past him to buy—
with our conscience burning holes
in the sleek, fat satin of our well-fed hearts—

and then some big old drunk Sally
came swinging past with her plastic sacks
and as she sang up a rough happiness
she'd scratched together somehow
she knocked his collection cup over
so all the loose change spilled out
with the faint jangle of lock-up keys
and a two-dollar coin shot away
like a panicked animal,
light ablaze on its skin

and another man chased it
into the traffic
where a courier van blared its horn
and the pursuer's toe tripped it as it spun
so it seemed to lunge sideways to dodge him
as it plunged through the grille
of a storm drain;
quenched like the flame
of a tiny Excalibur;
small miracle of compassion
withdrawn.

The Appointment

In the hospital's eye department, there are two identical art works framed on the wall. 'Why?' asks my seven-year-old.

'Perhaps it's like a game of spot the difference,' I answer. 'Or an eye department joke about double vision?'

'A super-bad one,' he says, giving me The Look.

We wait ages. Our books get tiring, so we start a game of hangman.

On the third round, my son finishes the gallows just as a young handcuffed detainee is ushered in by two cops. My son's hand freezes over the paper as the trio disappears behind a partition.

'J?' I guess, pretending all is normal, so my son won't be afraid. He draws a blank head.

The men reappear. 'FUCK that,' says the jailbird.

'Language,' warns the short cop as they escort the prisoner to the men's, where they have to wait in line.

'Ps and Qs,' I whisper. 'Mind your Ps and Qs.' My son looks puzzled.

'I?' is my next guess.

He pencils in another small circle.

'An eye for an I?' I ask. He throws The Look again. Then, in his clear, piping, piercing way, he asks, 'Are the police here 'cause justice is blind?'

I glance at the tattoos that flick like blue blades up the pale skinhead prisoner's neck.

The room plays deaf.

My son's name is called like a lifted sentence.

Removal

The bloodmark has been there for months:
like a bootprint tramped in by sadness,
or, as on a mariner's map, a small brown outcrop of loss.

Yet it cleans away so rapidly—
just a stiff brush, cold water, soap froth
and it evaporates like fog scrubbed off by noonday sun;
a pencilled problem quickly erased
when the debt worked out too great.

Those unkind words, though,
grind in their own red stain;
envy and cruelty spill bitter oils
that ruin the delicate barbs and barbules
of memory's once buoyant plumage.

Slander

Just say that for today, there are no have-tos.
Responsibility sets down its tools,
heels off its shoes, soaks its ankles
in the long, cool grass;
treads to the bed of dahlias, their pinwheel carnival,
lifts the invisible shutter from its inner ear;
lets the garden dot-dash the air's translucent sheet
in chords that morph with the breeze:
an earthy but elfin aria
on the edge of recorded language
like the songs of an isolate tribe
with no concept of covetousness, envy, or pride—
stop. Wreck the dream there.
If we knew such sweet, supernal music
how would we ever fully return
to our own clan's self-righteous jury?
Grief would be mind's lifelong quarantine.

Turn

It is so hard to be a good human in all the ways.
Time to go out to talk to the sunflowers, still visible through the white morning's mist. Close in, against the dark soil, each bloom gleams like the fired gold of a baritone sax inside the velvet lining of its case. Jackie says she loves the French for sunflowers; a phrase which travels two ways, like the word itself. *Tournesol*; flowers that turn towards the sun; flowers that turn the sun into flowers. *Tournesol*, they stand as a turnstile between seasons; between looking too far inward, and turning out to the city shivering in its thin, bright fabrics.

It is so hard to be a good human in all the ways.
Listen to what the sunflowers have to say. There is wisdom in their quiet faces.

My aunt says her grandson names her sunflowers: Tom, Tomasina, Little Tommy, Little D. So perhaps he agrees. He waters and waters their dark hearts, as if water were love and there could be no drowning in that. My own quiet sunpeople turn and seem to gaze this way. One is a black and watchful eye fringed with golden lashes. These others bow their brown cheeks, humble and furred as bees, deep in the meditation of plants. See the fingerprint whorl in the tawny deeps of this one; the curled petals of another, as if it retracts from some sting, a spurned child nursing itself. This other, a mother, hip-swaying, with diaphanous skirts whirling, as, with the hours, the sun leans lower through the mist. Here, a green, spiky little sister, still no bigger than a locket. There, a grandmother who might exclaim, 'Little rays of sunshine!' as she flings a meal's unused cutlery back into the drawer, the blades and tines spinning light to the ceiling as they fall. Yet another, a solemn grandfather, eyes cast down to his broad hands rough as emery boards as they worry at each other, their green veins delicately fuzzed with white prickles. And this one, cartwheeling on its leggy stem, like a seven-year-old allowed to rough it up again, now his arm is three weeks out of a cast, joy whirling his ragamuffin hair in a shaggy corona.

It is so hard to be a good human in all the ways.

The sunflowers cluster. They say gather the lustre of yourself and each other. They say burnish and finish and gleam, one to the other. The air around us now is ticking loud with late cicadas and crickets. All my sunpeople and I are the toothed cogs in a shimmering clock, letting time turn us, turn us, together.

Swarm

We heard our first bee swarm
in a stand of native trees
before we saw it; from the road thought
the thorned hum to be
the churn of a boat's engines idling.

Deep in the woods there were
single golden bullets whirling,
a twister of sun-dipped gravel,
and a massive, detached propeller
whose dark vibrating atoms
became a ghost's slung-off pelt;
then the melt of bees on the new hive
was living electric snow.

Your uncle said we had to fear attacks
only if the bees could sense our terror
so we clasped our dread tight against our skins
like diamonds, passports, cash
and as if they bought our forged innocence
the bees' swarm let us cross its border
to your uncle's hut where breath
rushed the honeycombs of our lungs.

Pivot

A skink swims its cursive over the gravel chips, vanishes

two dragonflies arabesque mid-air, are gone

cicadas disentangle from jasmine,
ricochet like chips of smashed green glass

The clouds in their mobile glyphs concur:

don't stay as you are

don't stay as you are

III

Selected Letters

Underneath the Fridge Magnet

Dear Fartypants and Coffeebreath
Dear Doodlebrain, Bumnuts,
Dogsbollocks and Spottyface

You never really loved me
So that's why I'm gone-burgers.
Please don't worry about it
not that you probably will
the kid in the middle
should come middle
or sometimes even first
but in my point of view
it's only mostly last.

I've got my backpack and my drink bottle
and a couple of books for if it gets boring
not that it probably will because runaways
have to think on their toes for their living
and there might be wild van-pirates
so I'll have to keep a constant look-out.
I've taken the one-eyed binoculars
that broke on the beach trip
and a warm layer like you always say.
Don't be angry but I've taken some of the cake
and I'll eat it too ha, ha.
Don't try to find me when I'm grown up.
You won't be able to because my alias
will be amazing. I'm making a list of cool ones.
If Julie or Tom go into my room, don't think I won't know.
Even if I die, my soul will know and you better believe
I've been practising karate in the park
so watch out because if they mess with my stuff

I could still come back—that is, if ever my ghost
gets done with running away.
Goodbye and thanks for the days
when it was good to have forgotten
I was once upon a time your only son.

Affidavit

He said, epistolary novels
sound like they should be about cowgirls.
Or at least, set where cowgirls shop—
like in a perfumery, or a dispensary.
An epistolary would stock a range
of compact fold-away travel guns
in multiple colours, with red-tipped slim-fit ammo
and the serving staff would be older, wiser cow-women,
whores with hearts of tooled leather, copper-jacketed lead.
You know, he'd always wondered,
once you could buy guns
that fit inside a handbag
why did women still let men
get away with so much violence?

She cocked
an eyebrow.
'What?' he said.
She licked her lips
as if some words
are swigs of strong grog.
She whispered—
Pistol-whipped.
She whispered—
Calibre.
She whispered—
Silencer.
Shit, he said.
So triggered.

Put your hands

right back

where I can

see them,

she said

.

Letter from Hamelin

The rats have moved into the attic; they slide inside the walls tricky as humidity. They have ignored the peanut-butter-laced traps, the cat, the poison bait and even the supersonic frequency device that's meant to Pied Piper them away. (A silent-to-humans security alarm, an opposite-to-dog-whistle, it's set at a pitch to call them off, like Mahler blasted out over shop doorways to repel loitering teens. Only these rats have settled in.)

The sound of them nags and sickens like a guilty conscience over everything we've left undone. They tap an audio memo that the whole globe's a boat fast-sinking because the rodents have had to come inside, to shelter from the non-summer. Sleet, hail, snow and rain fall all year round, every storm weather-bombs the records. The word *unseasonal* already seems obsolete. These are the chills of a planet running high fevers.

The sounds of munch, crack and thud in the ceiling are the earth's timbers breaking, the ice cap melting, the bones of all the endangered, bright and fearful symmetries collapsing to the ground.

They are at it night and day, this nibble and gnaw, an anxiety of rats, a fret of rats, a hazard, a startle reflex, a fright and flight and flight of rats. So hyperactive it is as if they're knocking back coffee beans on top of pseudoephedrine.

Freakish thought about vermin who do their animal work 24/7: not exactly the eating and breeding, though that is repellent enough, but the possibility of psychotic episodes induced by sleep deprivation. Not mine, though I do lie awake feeling more and more *1984*, but theirs. What would a rat with disordered thoughts do? Might it think it was an elephant, a wrecking ball, dress up in the kids' Batman gear, Darth Vader mask, would it try to fly? Or would it find a keyboard and try to type a tonally wrenched, discontinuous but mainly frightened letter to the world about the end times, while the end times keep on creeping on, as the rats slip in, the rats slip in, the rats slip in to the attic?

Letter from tomorrow's tomorrow and tomorrow

Dear time-mother and time-father

you gave us roars of wind spin, ice needles falling, blister sky. We think the small survivimals must store your voices, they cry out and they cry in, they cry out and they cry in; your names, do they keen them? For the survivimals sound even when first they are born as if your cinder-bones were red inside them and so early their spirits long for the leaping.

The light calls in dry splinters, burning. Stones on stones set scraping and rocking, rocks rocking, rocks rocking. The raw wind wishing, the boughs whipping and breaking, the sea rushes up rushes down, air forcing and pouring through night-dark waters splitting, how do we find our way to beforetimes?

When the bough downquakes hey hey when the baby wakes humma humma when the sky at last slants quiet and the day soft-croons in place, sudden times our skin-pulse wants—*tihei mauri ora!*—to pick up sticks, flick flax, knock bricks broken, beat hollow pipes rust-coated. Wants us to jump the flash jack, gas, gas, gas, la-la-la lay, lady-ay, sweetmusic-sweetmusic—bidda, budda, *boom*, bidda, budda *boom*

dit-dit-dit—dash—dash—dash—dit-dit-dit

Dear Friend

Dear friend I never see
but still think back to daily
often at the sun's draining tide
or now, say, when the poppies
on their long green wires
hum like an iPod's earbuds
and those small, dizzy gillespies the bees
pipe as if burning with the bluest blues
and my hands are in the tangled grasses
yanking hard at the roots of the undesired
until something inside falls so quiet
it is as if the mind climbs down to peer
deep into a still green pool of time
and wonder can gently wend its way to
—is it enough, that you're still there,
deeply held, all the sliding colours of you,
and the gestures like something
the packets of light choreographed
even deep inside the flowers' furred purses,
the seeds' foetal-curled sleep?
And when, not your words precisely,
but their slow, warm register burrs again
as if a breeze stirs an aerial,
or a man hums low in the past's far-off rooms,
as the inlet of memory flexes and fills,
flexes and fills, is that enough to go by?
Or shall I try again to write, to ask,
does this silence have anything to do with
sorry, I didn't, I never truly wanted,
that wasn't what those straw-gold
poppy-sway blue-barred days
ever betrayed at all?

Dear Adversity

I'm writing to ask
if the separate sorrows
we will give both sons
could be just enough
so when the large griefs come—
as we know they must come—
they can each take in the blow
not like a fist, but like a traveller
they see sodden in winter showers;
lay down the warm beds
of their hours;
withstand the toss and turn;
sweat and sleep off
despair's bone-deep wrack
so just a few pock-marks, pale lines
remain on the psyche's face,
as traces of when loss came
to run its course;
memory's red cells
already immunised
by today's small, live doses
of childhood tears.

Unlove

My friend who says her mind has frozen
My friend who says her mind has frozen—

My friend whose mind has frozen
sends me small gifts she says to keep her sane—
a cornflower blue watch;
a box carved of light with a green latch;
a grey egg she says will one day hatch
a small, exquisite monster, its teeth sharp as love.

'It will mark you for me,' she writes,
'Tiny cat nips, bee bites, gin stings—
its mouth filled with time's nettled patch
you would not pluck safe for me.'

Couldn't, I have to say to her, each time.
Couldn't. Body closed as a sugar snap pea.
Mind the silk-sheathed pulse in that body.
This love that thrives only in sun-winds pocketed
by cacti, rocks, hooves, scales:
in the feral thirsts of the near-alien,
not rippled mirrors of rains, lakes, streams.

C

up

id ne

eds contact le

nses and to reorganise both his belief system

and his physiological response to attachment relationships

by seeking some appropriate intensive therapeutic intervention

amirite?

.

Long Distance

Dear Dearest,

We dared it,
didn't we,
this nearness?

In its own way
courageous

for so costly
so ruinous

such closeness

apart.

The Tasti™ Taste Guarantee

At Tasti, our team are extremely proud of our delicious range of quality products, so if you think we could have done something better, or if there is anything you would like to know, please write ...

Dear Team

Thanks for the invitation.

I've just eaten one of your peanut-butter-flavoured Mega Nuts bars and I think you could have made the packaging less enticing.

Because I wasn't intending to eat your product—I was saving it for the kids.

And now I can feel the sticky caramel on my teeth, an odd sort of syrupy aftertaste of disappointment and gooey popcorn, and I'm writing this while deeply aware of the middle-aged pizza dough roll over my jogging shorts, and of my increasingly care-worn so-called willpower.

One bar is 10 per cent of my average daily calorie allowance.

I am profligate. I am ill-disciplined.

I am quite possibly your ideal clientele:

the kind who still partly believes that a muesli bar

is vaguely Swiss and healthy;

who thinks she can put your product in the kids' lunch boxes

and it will be both wholesome *and* exciting;

it will make them feel nurtured, central, and remembered;

it will encourage them to think of me fondly

when I am (body willing) in my eighties

counting the minutes till I can have another coffee

waiting for whatever sound postal delivery makes

in the non-dystopic future that many of us cling to

when seeing the thin blue lines on the pregnancy test stick

hoping right from that moment

that somewhere out there in the hurtling planet's

Vibro™ cities that survive because we all learnt

to recycle, conserve water, use cook-pots and screens

powered by the sun, the kids will sense

their prefrontal cerebral cortexes tingle and waltz
with the memory of opening the old ice-cream containers
we used as lunch boxes when the stupid flick-flack side-wing locks
on the expensive brand-name job-specific lunch boxes broke
and there, in its pack with the silver foil underskin
that shakes in the light like the sequins on a debut dancer's tutu,
was the chewy rectangle of protein and processed carbohydrates,
an understudy of mother's and father's love
that finally gets the chance to fill in and shine ...
and so the kids will write. Or call by. Or ring.

All of which I guess
is just to say
(hey WCW! Still got it!)
since you asked, I would like to know
how close-grained and sweet-glazed
is the happiness of the future
assuming there is happiness in the future?
Because sometimes, when I catch a glimpse
of time's webbed, oil-black wings,
its tangerine-stained, crazed-bullet teeth,
I'm so stunned and dread-run that even eating
a candy bar in Supergrain disguise
seems to be the opposite of inaction.

Dear Old Diaries

I'm sorry it's been so long.
Sorry I dumped all that on you.
I suppose you know I shredded and burnt one of you
in the aftermath of the bad lover
I wished had undergone a personality transplant?
Poor dead diary, punching bag, scratching post, voodoo doll,
ritual sacrifice, little strips blackening and bending,
contorted like small mouths howling in the waste-bin flames ...

Also, I guess you know that I mislaid one of you
when we moved house, twelve years ago?
It's bizarre how things turn out.
I mean, here I am, the long, slow reveal,
the 'in-the-middle-of (I hope) the-journey-of-my-life-
I-came-to-myself-within-a (please let it be only one) dark-wood',
the nameless abstract future
that once seemed to peer down
over the biro's gnomon shadow
through time's clear, curved bell jar
as if to find itself in the fine print:
and now mainly noticing
not the creak and labour of history,
the wonky frocks and bad habits, teen kicks,
blitherous superstitions, or made-for-TV morality—
but that little tousled head, bent as if in prayer;
though really more like a cat entranced
by the moving hieroglyphs of peculiar blue ants:
inky trails that lead to where it couldn't fathom,
still can't.

Joy

Do not use somersaults!
Remove all sharp objects from jumper!
Do not use when smoking!
Do not use with high blood pressure!
Do not use during pregnancy!
Do not use when suffering!
Use only bare foots!

Chain Mail

Bernie Gluckman, Texas
Daniel Luton, Balclutha
Cheryl Briar, Stoke Newington
Elif Smith, Istanbul
Emma Neale, Dunedin

Dear one

This charm has been created in the name of hope.
It will protect you like armour if you pass it on.
If you don't, we cannot be blamed for what fate befalls you.

One woman read this poem and passed it on.
Luck came to her in the form of many book vouchers, sympathetic friends,
and a shortlisting in an award with a cash prize.

Another woman read this poem but failed to pass it on.
We regret to say that the soul collector came to her in the night.
It lay beneath her bed, and, when she slept, checked the recycling bin for the poem,
found it there, then plucked the woman's soul for its dark album.

A man read this poem and he intended to pass it on, but left it in his briefcase
on a train. The train derailed, and the briefcase was destroyed. This man's full fate
is really too melancholy to relate, given—as is often the case with poems—you may
be reading deep in the marrow of night, with just a small desk lamp dozing
in its night cap for company beside you ...

So let us add emollient here to that burning urge to know the truth, and add that
further persons of fluid gender read this poem, circulated it, and to them came great
prosperity and—it must be said—many more wild and unaccountable poems.

Our advice is this. Within three days, make a copy of this poem, with your name at the bottom of the list that begins it. Wrap the page around another poem of your own as a charitable gift to the person named at the top of the list. (Now cross out that name.) Circulate this poem to five more friends.

Within ten days, your actions will have brought you bewilderment, laughter, curiosity, conversation, hope, and an abundance of poems.*

Will you strengthen the chain of human involvement? You must decide.
For with this last line, the charm is cast.

* (How many exactly will depend on postal services in your area.)

Dear Future, I'm afraid this is how I begin to lose you

I pictured a life jacket but I could only say diving gear.
I couldn't find a knife because my hands thought of spoons.
I wanted to slip away though I sang *Where's the book?*
I hunted for my wallet when I meant to recall the years.
I worried at the problem, but he could only see solutions:
when he said *Can you please explain?*
my reply was ghosting strangers on the stairs.

He wondered aloud if I even knew his name
yet at the sight of his bowed neck
regret finned to the evening's surface,
blue koi flickering at the stippling of rain.

Postcards Just Won't Cut It

Dear old man holding his cane halfway down like a marching baton, scything the air the way a child swings a stick at long, wild grass

Dear slightly floury, cottony February peach that helps us remember, wrist-dripping, shirt-staining real peaches

Dear exasperated established senior male author who thinks Track Changes are hell on earth but who keeps trying because of the indomitable human spirit plus deadlines

Dear little boy having his first day at a new educational programme, who had to roll a dice ten times this morning to make a decision, and who hides his head under a favorite bed-sheet he takes all around the house, and who likes to caress the small rabbit's ears he fashions out of the two best corners

Dear elderly, thin woman speed-walking like a stalk of lavender blown along upright in a great wind

Dear creased white net curtain billowing and reminding me of another botched poem with a white net curtain billowing which reminded me then of my father's death and which even now makes me want to cradle his mid-thirties wet swimming-pool head from that '70s photo where he embraces my little sister, his goofy grin as if he's the benign human incarnation of a bear with its stomach full of salmon

Dear patterned steeplechase of light and shade through the creeper, the deck fencing, the ranch-slider, now showing up on the sandy, crumby, balding rug

Dear man who can hold my gaze now though I suspect it was something close to prideful, and so therefore shameful, in his background, which in fact we have never discussed

Dear woman whose colour sense in everything from intricate stitchwork to what dishcloth and coffeepot should sit side by side is like an optical cadenza

Dear twig from the Bullock Track used as a bookmark in Knausgaard's *A Man in Love*

Dear hash brown chef of the hashtag generation

Dear eight-year-old yodelling loudly in the Botanic Garden toilets to voodoo away ghosts, spiders and bogey men and exiting again with a soap-foam beard

Dear small girl with a tiara over her baseball cap and lime-green sandals snap-domed with silver Mercury wings

Dear crank caller, too shy to even dial the number, but composing devastating witticisms under his breath on the bus

Dear middle-aged man on unexpected weight-loss bout caused by love for another man's life, no that's not a typo for wife

Dear teenager plodding uphill dreaming of swimming from shore to shore and wanting to be reincarnated as music

Dear strand of jazz piano falling through the air like a string of silver lights

    How I wish
    I could stay

Economy of Style

Due to circumstances
we should have foreseen
the exquisite poems
we had hoped for
have not been composed.
We regret to say
until further notice
this space remains closed.

Envoi

Reader, wait up!
Please, don't turn away like that.
I'm sure we can work this out.

Let's just sit here a while,
feel the light pour
like silent cataracts,
its radiant wash joining us,
two dots of consciousness
particles we might name
the Vladimirs and Estragons
of trust.

Acknowledgements and Notes

Thanks are due to the editors of the following publications where some of these works (or versions of them) have appeared or are forthcoming: *Angry Old Man* (US); *A Poetry Shelf for Paula Green*; *Bath Flash Fiction Anthology 2018* (UK); *Bridport Prize Anthology 2018* (UK); *The Cerurove* (US); *The Friday Poem: 100 New Zealand poems* (Luncheon Sausage Books, 2018); *Geometry*; *HeadStuff* (Ireland); *Landfall*; *London Grip* (UK); *NB Magazine*; NZ Poetry Shelf; *Otago Daily Times*; Phantom Billstickers poetry posters; *Poetry Daily* (US); *Poetry Ireland Review*; *Poetry New Zealand Yearbook 2018*; *Reflex Flash Fiction*; *The Spinoff*; *Sport*; Verbatim Found Poetry; and *Ware Poets Prize Anthology 2018* (UK).

'The Appointment' was longlisted in the Summer Reflex Fiction International Competition 2018. 'Still' and 'Mère-mare' were both shortlisted in the 2017 Bridport Prize Poetry category, judged by Lemn Sissay; and 'Courtship' was highly commended in the 2018 Bridport Prize Flash Fiction category, judged by Monica Ali.

'Dear Future, I'm afraid this is how I begin to lose you' was shortlisted in the National Memory Day Competition, UK, November 2018. 'Doorway' was commended in the Ware Poets Open Competition, UK, 2018. 'The Local Pool' won third place in the Bath Flash Fiction Award 2018, judged by Nuala O'Connor (Nuala Ní Chonchúir).

'So Buttoned Up' was selected for *Best New Zealand Poems 2018* (edited by Fiona Farrell), IIML.

'Withdrawn' was originally commissioned for the 'Poets on Place' event at the Dunedin Writers & Readers Festival 2017, produced by Ian Loughran.

'Letter from tomorrow's tomorrow and tomorrow' was originally prompted by *Tautitotito (Disputation Songs): Other genealogies of Aotearoa New Zealand music* (2018), produced by Alex Taylor and Celeste Oram. The producers asked for letters 'written in a speculative future and addressed to the present day' to address several questions, one of which was 'How has music and sound shaped the histories of Aotearoa New Zealand, and how will it continue to shape our futures?'

'So Buttoned Up' uses the two opening lines from Stephen Bett's 'For Love of You' as its own opening lines. 'my mother in this way mixing me wings and tongue' takes its title from a couplet in 'Red', by Paula Green, from her book *Chrome* (Auckland University Press, Auckland, 2000).

'Joy' is a treated found poem; the text is rearranged from a Big Bounce Trampoline safety notice.

Grateful acknowledgement is also due to Creative New Zealand, who funded me to write a novel, part of which rebelled and ran off into poems.